PREFACE

This study is based on open source research into the scope of Asian organized crime and terrorist activity in Canada during the period 1999 to 2002, and the extent of cooperation and possible overlap between criminal and terrorist activities in that country. The analyst examined those Asian organized crime syndicates that direct their criminal activities at the United States via Canada, namely crime groups trafficking heroin from Southeast Asia, groups engaging in the trafficking of women, and groups committing financial crimes against U.S. interests. The terrorist organizations examined were those that are viewed as potentially planning attacks on U.S. interests.

The analyst researched the various holdings of the Library of Congress, the Open Source Information System (OSIS), other press accounts, and various studies produced by scholars and organizations. Numerous other online research services were also used in preparing this study, including those of NGOs and international organizations.

TABLE OF CONTENTS

KEY FINDINGS

- Despite several border concerns that need to be addressed, the sheer length of the U.S.-Canadian border, at over 5,500 miles and containing vast zones of virtually nonexistent border demarcation, make it unlikely that any amount of funding can entirely address the border issue. Canadian authorities should therefore emphasize port security and immigration policy as a means of ensuring that Asian organized crime and terrorist groups cannot enter Canada in the first place.

- Since September 11, 2001, Canada has taken significant steps toward combating terrorist activities by passing laws and allocating funds for securing the U.S.-Canada border, tightening refugee policies, and detecting and deferring the financing of terrorist activities. However, because these initiatives have been in effect for less than two years, it is difficult to accurately gauge their effectiveness.

- In 2000, about 50 terrorist groups and more than 350 members reportedly used Canada as a base from which to conduct their activities.

- Canada's 2001 *Anti-Terrorism Act* has dealt a serious legal blow to terrorist organizations that have relied on Canada as a financial resource by raising funds for their causes. However, the list of terrorist organizations banned under the Act is currently 16, and includes fewer than half of the groups listed on a similar list organized by the U.S. State Department.

- In recent years, some experts have noted that non-triad organizations constitute the majority of Asian organized crime groups. It appears likely that many Asian organized crime syndicates exaggerate their links with triads in order to inspire fear. In actuality, these groups often consist of business entrepreneurs who may employ triad members to better pursue illicit activities. Therefore, it is difficult to thoroughly examine Asian organized crime without looking beyond individual triads.

- The Big Circle Boys gang has demonstrated the greatest expansion in Canada since its presence was detected there in the late 1980s. With cells present in cities throughout North America, and a willingness to cooperate with ethnically diverse groups, the Big Circle Boys have become extensively involved in the Southeast Asia heroin trade and are responsible for a high percentage of the counterfeit credit cards in North America.

- The 14K triad is the fastest growing group in Canada and has a presence in New York and other U.S. cities.

- Vietnamese organized crime groups in Canada are expanding rapidly in high-technology crimes and are believed to be involved in the trafficking of women. Their extensive networking activities have led to fear that such groups eventually will be organized into formal and structured groups.

- Although terrorist organizations use some of the same techniques for generating revenue as organized crime groups, and many experts agree that complicity among these disparate groups exists, open-source research did not reveal many examples of this cooperation.

- Faced with the likely spread of Asian organized crime groups and given border porosity and immigration laws, for the foreseeable future Canada will continue to serve as an ideal transit point for crime groups to gain a foothold in the United States. The new *Immigration and Refugee Protection Act*, which took effect in June 2002, may be successful at addressing some of the issues regarding immigration to Canada.

INTRODUCTION

For the past three years, information has revealed a proliferation of Asian organized crime groups in Canada. Since September 11, 2001, the Canadian government has paid increasing attention to terrorist organizations and has initiated several changes in government policy to tighten border security and combat terrorism. The success of these new policies is yet to be fully evaluated. Several factors continue to support the development of these criminal and terrorist groups' use of Canada as either a transit point or base from which to conduct their activities in the United States.

In April 2003, the U.S. State Department published its annual *Patterns of Global Terrorism* report. Although Canada receives an overall positive rating, certain aspects of Canadian policy were found to be counterproductive to U.S. security. The porosity of the Canadian border is worrisome. In addition, some U.S. law enforcement officers have expressed worry that Canadian privacy laws designed to protect Canadian citizens and landed immigrants from governmental intrusions and insufficient funding for the law enforcement community inhibit "a fuller and more timely exchange of information and response to requests for assistance" from their U.S. counterparts.[1]

U.S.-CANADIAN BORDER ASSESSMENT

Commercial Activity

The U.S-Canadian border stretches approximately 5,500 miles. It is the longest undefended border in the world, as well as the busiest; each country is the other's largest trading partner. In terms of proximity, about eighty percent of the Canadian population lives within two hours of the U.S.-Canadian border, making it an ideal staging ground to conduct activities in the United States.[2] With the advent of the North American Free Trade Agreement (NAFTA) in 1994, the past decade has seen a significant increase in trans-border commercial activity. Canadian exports to the United States rose from US$121b in 1991 to US$242b in 2000. As an example of the continuing expansion of commercial activity, each day approximately 7,000

---

[1] United States Department of State, *Patterns of Global Terrorism, 2002* (Washington: 2003). <http://www.state.gov>
[2] Jonathan Weisman, "Cigarette Black Market Feared; Canadian Tax Increase Led to Smuggling and Organized Crime Rivalry; Industry Complicity Alleged," *The Sun* [Baltimore], May 10, 1998.

trucks cross the border at the Ambassador Bridge, connecting Detroit, Michigan with Windsor, Canada. The Ambassador Bridge is just one of 113 designated land crossings, 62 of which were unguarded at night as of October 2001.[3]

Contributing to the problem, sparsely populated mountainous regions, prairie, and forest where in many places border demarcation is virtually nonexistent, comprise the vast expanse of the border. In comparison to Mexico, which has approximately 9,000 Customs, Immigration and Naturalization Service and Border Control personnel guarding the 2,000-mile United States-Mexican border, only 965 such U.S. personnel were guarding the Canadian border as of October 2001, and only 2400 Canadian Customs personnel were on duty.[4] According to a September 2002 article in *The News Tribune* [Tacoma, WA], only 346 U.S. Border Control agents were assigned to the U.S.-Canadian border, including the border with Alaska. This number averages out to one agent for every 16 miles, and represents an increase of only 15 people since September 11, 2001.[5] Given these conditions, the porosity of the U.S.-Canadian border represents a continued problem.

Akwesasne Reservation

Adding to the issue of border porosity is the use of the Akwesasne reservation as an illegal border crossing. The reservation, consisting of 14,000 acres, is home to the St. Regis Mohawk Indians. The territory reaches from Cornwall, Ontario, and Massena, New York, along 25 miles of the St. Lawrence River channels and 20 islands, to just north of Vermont.[6]

The Mohawk Nation Council controls the entire expanse of the reservation's territory. Although not recognized by either the government of the United States or Canada, the council has demanded and has been granted the right of the Mohawk people to have freedom of movement across the U.S.-Canadian border, as well as the right to transport goods across the border without controls or payment of taxes. This demand was granted with the condition that non-native people are not allowed to take advantage of the rights of movement and tax-free

---

[3] Statement of James W. Ziglar Before the Senate Appropriations Committee on Treasury and General Government, October 3, 2001. <http://www.immigration.gov/graphics/aboutus/congress/testimonies/2001/10_03_01.pdf>
[4] Jack Kelly, "Quick, Easy Crossing a Thing of the Past at Canadian Border," *Pittsburgh Post-Gazette*, October 14, 2001.
[5] Sean Robinson, "Northern Border Exposure; Increased Presence of Terrorists in Canada, Staffing Shortage at U.S. Border Patrol a Bad Combination," *The News Tribune* [Tacoma], September 29, 2002.
[6] Jeffrey Robinson, *The Merger: How Organized Crime Is Taking Over Canada and the World* (McClelland & Stewart Inc: 1999), 58.

trade. Despite this requirement, the region is used as an illegal border crossing for Asian organized crime groups, among others and, therefore, constitutes one of the primary gaps in border security.[7]

Although U.S. and Canadian authorities have the right to inspect the land for illegal contraband or persons crossing without permission, this right is often not exercised. Instead, a militant group of Akwesasne, equipped with stockpiles of small arms, acts as defenders of the land, exercising control over the individuals entering their territory.[8] The group receives its funding almost exclusively from the proceeds of criminal activities. The Walpole Island and the Niagara area also continue to be used by Asian organized crime groups as a convenient route to smuggle both contraband and people across the border, due to its geographic location between Ontario and Michigan at the mouth of the St. Clair River.[9]

Immigration and Refugee Policy

Canada's immigration policy and entrepreneur program allow foreign nationals to enter the country with relative ease and become Canadian residents, thereby positioning themselves for easy access to the United States. Each year approximately 300,000 people are allowed entry into Canada, twice the number per capita that the United States allows in.[10] In addition, few restrictions apply to countries of origin for persons seeking entry into Canada. Unlike the visa waiver program in the United States, which grants entry without a visa to residents of only 27 countries, Canada grants visa-free entry to residents of nearly 60 countries. This number includes Greece, Mexico, South Korea, and Saudi Arabia. Canada relies on paper identification for immigrants, forged versions of which are available on the black market for roughly $1,000.[11] Those found to be misrepresenting themselves at the border do not face any ban. They are merely turned away and can attempt to re-enter the country immediately.[12] Asian criminal groups, especially those from China, Hong Kong, Macau, and Taiwan, as well as terrorist

---

[7] LaVerle Berry, *Russian Organized Crime and the Global Narcotics Trade* (Washington: Library of Congress, Federal Research Division), March 2002.
[8] Ibid.
[9] Criminal Intelligence Service Canada, *Annual Report on Organized Crime in Canada 2001*, Website: <http://www.cisc.gc.ca/AnnualReport2001/Cisc2001/coverpage2001.html>
[10] John Berlau, "Canada Turns into Terrorist Haven," *Insight on the News* [Washington], June 24, 2002. <http://www.insightmag.com/news/254290 html>
[11] Jim Lynch, "A New Bond at Border," *The Oregonian* [Portland], October 28, 2001, A1.
[12] Ibid.

groups, exploit these policies.[13] A report in the *Hong Kong Kuang Chiao Ching* indicated that Chinese organized crime groups from these regions are increasingly using Canada as a base because of their ability to obtain legal residency in Canada relatively easily and then freely enter the United States.[14]

Canada's refugee policy has been very welcoming since the mid-80s. It was then that the Canadian Supreme Court broadened the definition of "refugee" by guaranteeing a hearing for anyone entering the country claiming to be a refugee, even if that person could provide no documentation. The new *Immigration and Refugee Protection Act*, which took effect in June 2002, does not challenge this right to a hearing without documentation, although it does implement a number of changes that make it more difficult for terrorists or international criminals to gain entry to or stay in Canada. The new Act requires a reasonable explanation for a lack of documentation and penalizes the failure to take reasonable steps to obtain such documents. In contrast to the situation in the United States, however, people rarely are detained because of lack of identifying papers. Even under the newly passed *Immigration and Refugee Act*, appeals are automatically heard.[15] Additional changes to the law include measures designed to detect fraudulent asylum applications and significantly harsher penalties for those caught smuggling people into Canada.[16]

The process of determining a person's eligibility for refugee status can take years, and even if a refugee claim is denied claimants often can stay in Canada if they declare that they will be put in danger when returning to their native country.[17] While awaiting a scheduled hearing, a refugee claimant is eligible for welfare or employment and is covered by the national healthcare system. Refugee claimants may also avail themselves of the public education system. The number of refugee claimants was 44,000 in 2001, up from 22,000 just three years before; the number of refugees allowed entry each year is now approximately 30,000.[18] However, possibly 60 percent of all claimants possess insufficient documentation or no documentation at all.

---

[13] "Asian Organized Crime," *International Crime Threat Assessment*, 2000.
<http://www.fas.org/irp/threat/pub45270chap3.html#r14>
[14] Hsiao Yang, "China Steps Up Its Crackdown On the Mob And Severely Punishes Mob Leaders," *Hong Kong Kuang Chiao Ching*, February 16, 2001 (FBIS Document CPP20010216000052).
[15] "Asian Organized Crime," *International Crime Threat Assessment*, 2000.
<http://www.fas.org/irp/threat/pub45270chap3.html#r14>
[16] Citizenship and Immigration Canada, *Immigration and Refugee Protection Act*.
<http://www.cic.gc.ca/english/irpa/>
[17] Berlau.
[18] Kelly.

Hence, many just disappear, often skipping their asylum hearings, and enter the United States illegally. Currently over 25,000 arrest warrants are outstanding for those people who have skipped their asylum hearings.[19]

The case of Lai Changxing serves as a rather typical example of such claimants. Lai entered Canada in 1999 after fleeing China to avoid arrest for having bribed thousands of Chinese officials with cash and women to protect a crime ring that smuggled an estimated US$6.4 billion in stolen vehicles, crude oil, weapons, and computers into Fujian province through the port of Xiamen.[20] Lai's fake passport was not identified when he entered and settled in Canada, and he began associating immediately with Asian organized crime groups. Lai was apprehended on November 23, 2000, after Chinese officials had urged his arrest for 15 months, but he has not been extradited. Lai is likely to be executed for his crimes if he returns.

It is believed that the Big Circle Boys gang and the Leun Kung Lok triad may have assisted Lai in transferring his assets to Canada after fleeing China.[21] Lai currently is out of jail after an immigration adjudicator found in June 2002 that despite his failed refugee claim and unsubstantiated RCMP reports that he was trying to obtain fake passports, he was unlikely to flee the country.[22]

Canadian Ports

According to a March 2002 article in the *National Post*, a Canadian Senate committee on national security, which met in February 2002, identified Canada's ports as a breeding ground for organized crime and terrorism.[23] In 1996, when the government began to disband the port police service, private security companies began assuming security responsibilities at Canadian ports. The senate committee reported that 36 percent of employees in charge of going over manifest lists for cargo containers at the port of Montreal, 39 percent of the dock workers at

---

[19] Berlau.

[20] Tom Cohen, "Canada Denies Bail to Chinese Smuggler," *Pittsburgh Post*, December 6, 2000, A5.

[21] "Triad Link Alleged in Transfer of Millions to Accused Smuggler Lai," *Beijing China Daily* [Beijing], December 4, 2000. (FBIS Document CPP20001204000045).

[22] Petti Fong, "Alleged Smuggler Allowed Home: Lai Changxing and Wife Released Despite Claims About False Passports," *The Vancouver Sun*, June 29, 2002.

[23] The Canadian senate report also recommends that Canada increase military spending by $4 billion a year and increase the size of the military from 20,000 to 75,000. Canada currently spends approximately 1.2 percent of its GDP on defense, roughly half of what other NATO members allocate.

Halifax, and 54 percent of the dock workers at the Charlottetown port had criminal records.[24] In addition, several ports do not have adequate identification requirements for employers nor do they have adequate security fencing.

Organized crime groups reportedly exercise great control over Canadian ports and have been cited as major conduits for drug smuggling, the export and import of stolen automobiles, and the theft of cargo. Officials fear that terrorists could use the ports to smuggle a weapon of mass destruction into the country.[25] The committee additionally reported that the Chrétien government had been receiving warnings on the state of Canada's ports for six years, but continued to ignore the advice of law enforcement officials.

Effects of September 11

The terrorist attacks on the United States in September 2001 were a catalyst for bringing the issues of Canadian immigration policy and U.S.-Canadian border security to the forefront. In October 2001, Canada implemented its *Anti-Terrorism Plan*, and in December 2001 its *Anti-Terrorism Act* entered into force. Among other things, these two initiatives are designed to prevent terrorists from getting into Canada, secure the U.S.-Canada border, identify terrorist activities, and detect and deter the financing of terrorist activities.[26] Subsequent changes to the Canadian *Immigration and Refugee Protection Act* in June 2002 seek to remove some of the heretofore less stringent refugee policies by allowing for the removal of security threats sooner and the imposition of harsher penalties for people smuggling, as well as for people using or selling forged documents. US$200 million has been allocated to improve the screening of foreigners.[27] The Canadian *Budget 2001*, passed in December 2001, allocates CDN$7.7b over the next five years to provide funding for these initiatives. Other initiatives include the *Canada-U.S. Smart Border Declaration* and accompanying *Action Plan for Creating a Secure and Smart Border,* signed on December 12, 2001, and designed to protect the CDN$1.9 billion dollars garnered daily from legitimate border trade while ensuring its security from illicit activities.

---

[24] James Baxter, "Current Senate Report Said To Confirm 1996 Warnings on Canadian Port Security," *National Post* [Toronto], March 19, 2002 (FBIS Document EUP20020304000245).

[25] Allan Thompson, "Canadian Senate Report Says Ports 'Fertile Ground' for Terrorists, Notes Workers' Criminal Records," *The Toronto Star*, March 2, 2002 (FBIS Document EUP20020304000245).

[26] Canada Embassy in Washington, "*Canada's Actions Against Terrorism Since September 11th*," Washington, D.C.: 2003. <http://www.canadianembassy.org/border/backgrounder-en.asp>

[27] Berlau.

This goal is to be achieved through enhanced coordination and by implementing border security systems that identify the most prevalent security risks to both countries' infrastructures in terms of people and goods, while assuring the free and expeditious flow of people and commerce across the border.[28]

Although geared toward preventing terrorist organizations from pursuing their objectives, these measures also hinder members of Asian organized crime groups that seek entry into the United States or Canada, as well as helping to prevent perpetration of cross border criminal activities. Nevertheless, the relatively recent implementation of these initiatives makes it unclear whether they will be successful at addressing the problems.

Other issues also have been raised. A June 3, 2002 article in *Insight on the News* points out that certain changes to the Canadian *Immigration and Refugee Protection Act* may prove counterproductive in the fight against terrorism. Previously, the courts were able to exercise discretion regarding which refugee cases would be heard on appeal; amendments to the act now guarantee that any appeal made will be heard automatically, a change that has been criticized as enabling persons with false claims to remain within the country and jeopardize security.[29]

ASIAN ORGANIZED CRIME

Background

Unlike traditional organized crime groups such as the Italian La Cosa Nostra, Asian organized crime groups, including both those groups that were established in Canada and those that originate abroad but have members operating in Canada, lack a set structure at the operational level even if a hierarchy exists at the organizational level. This is true of Chinese tongs, gangs, and other organized crime networks. The traditional Chinese triad societies, originally secret societies, some of which have existed for centuries, also operate in this fashion at the operational level. The Chinese triads, which have offices, ranks, and oaths, use this hierarchical structure to bond members, but not to dictate their activities. However, if a parent organization exists, these groups still maintain certain loyalties to that organization. This loyalty

---

[28] Canadian Embassy, "*Canada's Actions Against Terrorism Since September 11th,*" Washington, D.C.: 2003. <http://www.canadianembassy.org/border/backgrounder-en.asp>
[29] Berlau.

is often expressed in terms of assistance to members who are relocating and in pursuit of profitable ventures for members, when it is convenient.

Even when part of a specific well-known group, such as the Big Circle Boys, for example, members often operate in small, cell-structured groups or partnerships, if not independently, when engaging in illegal activities. Subsequent to the achievement of a particular goal, these partnerships often are dissolved. As documented by the 2002 annual report of the Criminal Intelligence Service Canada (CISC), these groups demonstrate "structural fluidity and flexibility."[30] It is not at all uncommon for members and associates of these groups to conduct numerous dissimilar criminal activities, often with different groups simultaneously, be they ethnically homogenous or heterogeneous.[31] It is because of this decentralization that specific details on individuals and groups are often unavailable, at least in open source research materials. In contrast to the Cosa Nostra, which is organized in a pyramid structure, making it possible for law enforcement to trace the organization to its highest level, Asian organized crime groups are organized more as autonomous mini-pyramids, with small cells and mini-bosses dictating the actions of only their particular cell. More sophisticated organized crime groups include individuals who engage in frequent travel, both domestically and internationally, often for the purposes of evading law enforcement.[32] Established groups routinely use youth and street gangs as a labor resource as well as a means to expand their activities.

Canada's Asian crime groups are more complicated to combat than groups such as the Italian Cosa Nostra because of historical and geographical factors. Asian organized crime groups place high priority on ethnicity for membership in their organizations. This fact is especially true for the more traditionally oriented Chinese triads. There are few, if any, accounts of non-Asian members being accepted in their networks. Hence, given the lack of Asians in U.S. and Canadian law enforcement, the networks are difficult to infiltrate.

U.S. and Canadian law enforcement authorities presently are unable to strike at the core of many triads, which often are located in countries where broad cooperation between law enforcement officials currently does not exist. And in many cases, the independent and cell-structured nature of most Asian organized crime groups makes it unlikely that destruction of the

---

[30] Criminal Intelligence Service Canada, *Annual Report on Organized Crime Canada* (Ottawa: 2002) <http://www.cics.gc.ca>
[31] Ibid.
[32] Yiu Kong Chu, *The Triads as Business* (New York: St. Edmundsbury Press 2000).

central authority of the more organized triad groups would have any substantial detrimental effect on operations in Canada and in the United States. The presence of various cells from the same organization in different cities or countries also gives these groups contacts that they can trust and do business with. These cells have proven to be of great advantage to a criminal group like Big Circle Boys, for example, allowing the group to combine its various assets and expertise for the perpetration of transnational crimes.

In recent years, some experts have noted that non-triad groups constitute the majority of Asian organized crime activities. Since 1994, three years before the return of Hong Kong to Chinese rule, crimes perpetrated by triads have not risen above 3.8 percent in Hong Kong as a result of the efforts of law enforcement.[33] Organized crime groups may exaggerate their links with triads in order to inspire fear. As a result, it has become increasingly difficult to determine whether triads or more contemporary syndicates commit transnational crime. Therefore, law enforcement's view regarding triad involvement at all levels may need to be reexamined.[34] Furthermore, the formal links between the triads in Hong Kong and their members abroad are becoming increasingly questionable. The links may be only temporary and exist to facilitate taking advantage of certain opportunities, rather than being institutionalized.[35] However, triad societies do play vital roles in transnational organized crime activities.

Types of Crime

Heroin Trafficking

Background

The United States-Canada Border Drug Threat Assessment of December 2001 estimates that 95 percent of all heroin entering Canada originates in Southeast Asia.[36] Chinese organized crime groups in Canada almost exclusively traffic heroin produced in Southeast Asia, primarily originating in parts of Burma, Laos, and Thailand, known as the "Golden Triangle" region.

---

[33] John Hill, "Triad Societies Seek Increased Opportunities as China Opens Up," *Jane's Intelligence Review*, January 1, 2003. <http://www.janes.com>

[34] Chu, 119.

[35] Hill.

[36] Criminal Intelligence Service Canada, *Annual Report on Organized Crime Canada* (Ottawa: 2002). <http://www.cics.gc.ca>

Canadian intelligence additionally suggests that Burma is becoming a major source of ecstasy and that Asian organized crime groups soon will move to exploit the situation.[37]

According to the Criminal Intelligence Service Canada (CISC), all major heroin seizures in 2000 and 2001 involved Asian organized crime groups, although these groups may link with other groups to facilitate their activities. The report further found that Southeast Asian heroin usually enters Canada through Vancouver, Toronto, or Montreal via international airports and major British Columbia marine ports. The CISC also reports that Asian organized crime groups use the northern half of Saskatchewan for the importation of heroin and cocaine from British Columbia and Alberta. In addition, the CISC reports that Chinese and Vietnamese drug syndicates based out of Edmonton, Alberta, and Calgary now have established a permanent presence in these regions and that Ontario groups are continually involved in the large-scale importation of heroin.[38]

The presence of these groups in Canada is a threat to the United States. The groups that smuggle heroin into the United States often operate on both sides of the border and control distribution.[39] Furthermore, several organized crime groups overseas are involved in shipping heroin to Canada for the very purpose of exploiting the porosity of the U.S.-Canadian border.[40] Heroin trafficking, in particular, involves the cooperation of various groups at different levels to get the product to its final destination. For example, street gangs often act as enforcers who are, in turn, supported by more established and powerful groups.[41]

These trafficking groups are independent and diverse, composed of both triads and other criminal organizations. Although individual triad members reportedly are involved in trafficking heroin to the United States through Canada, the triads as organizations do not control the trade.[42] Triad membership is more a prerequisite for sellers to gain permission to sell drugs at the street level. No such membership seems to be required for entering the international drug market. The October 2001 discovery of a highly organized Asian syndicate with direct links to Canada

---

[37] United States Department of Justice, National Drug Intelligence Center, *Heroin Distribution in Three Cities* (November 2000). <http://www.usdoj.gov/ndic/pubs/648/intro.htm>
[38] Criminal Intelligence Service Canada, *Annual Report on Organized Crime Canada* (Ottawa: 2001). <http://www.cics.gc.ca>
[39] Royal Canadian Mounted Police, Criminal Intelligence Program, "Drug Situation in Canada – 1999" (Ottawa: 2000). <http://www rcmp-grc.gc.ca>
[40] Ibid.
[41] Ibid.
[42] Chu, 119.

exemplifies the lack of triad control over the drug trafficking industry. Approximately 430,000 tablets of ecstasy with a value of US$30m were discovered heading toward Australia; this cache was the second largest seizure of amphetamines ever recorded.[43] Although one of the men arrested reportedly had links to the Sun Yee On triad, the ecstasy movement was not a triad operation. From the magnitude of this seizure it is apparent that international crime syndicates have real power in the drug trade, despite only tangential identification with a major triad.

It is not uncommon for a member of one triad to team up with another triad member and work for the leader of a heroin smuggling group who is not a member of any triad at all.[44] The situation is viewed as a private business transaction. Still, triad membership can be essential for purposes of networking and the development of criminal relationships based on trust.

It should also be noted that no consensus exists on the degree of triad involvement in the Canadian drug trade, and some officials believe that the triads control the market.[45]

Heroin-Related Activity Affecting U.S. and Canadian Interests: 1999-2002

Heroin from Southeast Asian and China has been entering Western Canada for many years on its way to North American markets. In January 1999, *The Vancouver Sun* reported the Royal Canadian Mounted Police's (RCMP) seizure of 70 kilograms of heroin in Richmond Country and two Mercedes Benz automobiles, one in Toronto and one in Vancouver. Five people connected to the seizure were arrested in Toronto, Richmond County, British Columbia, and Hong Kong. According to the report, the police claimed that those arrested were part of a major organized crime group that was stockpiling Golden Triangle heroin in Vancouver before shipping it out to points throughout North America.[46] In June 1999, the RCMP broke up a global drug smuggling syndicate that was controlled out of Hong Kong and trafficked heroin from the Golden Triangle. With profits estimated in the multimillions, the group shipped narcotics to Vancouver, where triad groups in Canada then transported the heroin to the rest of the North American market. The drug smuggling syndicate was discovered in December 1997; Vancouver detectives reported that it had been in operation for a number of years prior to its discovery.

---

[43] Neil Mercer, "$30 M Drug Seizure Cracks Crime Syndicate," *The Sydney Morning Herald*, October 18, 2001. (Lexis Nexis Document)
[44] Chu, 110.
[45] "Wa Link to Triad Confirmed," *The Bangkok Post*, December 22, 2000.
[46] David Hogben, "Warehouse in Richmond Yields 70 Kilos of High-Grade Heroin: Arrest of Five a Major Blow to Organized Crime, Police Say," *The Vancouver Sun*, January 20, 1999, B1. (LexisNexis Document)

Over 30 Hong Kong residents were arrested in Canada and the United States.[47] A number of individuals belonging to the syndicate also were charged with being linked to extortion and credit card fraud and were suspected of links to Macau triads.[48]

Law enforcement officials in the United States and Canada cooperated in numerous police actions to curtail illegal narcotics activity. In June 1999, Project E-PAGE resulted in the arrest of 28 members of an Asian organized crime group active in British Columbia and various cities within the United States, Thailand, Hong Kong, and Burma. Law enforcement authorities in the United States recovered 6.3 kilograms of heroin and thwarted several planned conspiracies to import additional heroin to North America.[49] In August and September of 2000, a year-long investigation, named Project Occlude, resulted in the seizure of 57 kilograms of heroin and other narcotics in Toronto; the estimated street value of the seized narcotics was US$142.5 million. After arriving in Vancouver from China's Guangdong province, the heroin had been shipped by rail to Toronto. According to an article in the *Ottawa Citizen*, no link was made to any of the triads at the trial of the apprehended suspects, but the volume of the narcotics in question suggested that a large network was involved.[50] In 2000, the RCMP also seized 99 kilograms of heroin in Vancouver with an estimated street value of approximately US$104m. A Hong Kong resident named Chak Nam Chan was found guilty and sentenced to 14 years in jail.[51] The *RCMP Drug Situation in Canada-2000* report notes that the importers of this heroin engaged in criminal enterprises other than drug trafficking while waiting for the price of heroin in Canada to rise to profitable levels.

Narcotics dealers in China do not limit themselves to heroin dealing. On April 12, 2001, according to the RCMP *Drug Situation in Canada – 2001* report, 48.7 kilograms of Southeast Asian heroin were discovered in two containers of pineapples that arrived in Vancouver. One of the containers was scheduled to be shipped on to Markham, Ontario. The containers were loaded

---

[47] "Canadian Police: Huge Heroin Deals funded From Hong Kong," *Hong Kong South China Sunday Morning Post in English*, June 27, 1999 (FBIS Document CPP19990628000046).

[48] Lori Culbert, "Poolhall Operator Linked to Heroin Ring: A Vancouver Man Is Among 32 People who Have Been Charged in Connection with Two Cases that Span Several Continents," *The Vancouver Sun* June 24, 1999.

[49] Royal Canadian Mounted Police, Criminal Intelligence Program. "Drug Situation in Canada – 1999." (Ottawa 2000). <http://www rcmp-grc.gc.ca>

[50] Shannon Kari, "Mother, 50, Sentenced to 17 Years for Smuggling Heroin, Amphetamines: Son, 22, Confesses to Lesser Charge," *The Ottawa Citizen*, June 1, 2002. (LexisNexis Document)

[51] Andy Ivens, "14 Years for Trafficker Nabbed in Heroin Bust, " *The Vancouver Province*, February 2, 2001.

in Hangpu, China. The shipment also contained 250 packets of phenyl acetone, a precursor chemical for the preparation of amphetamine and methamphetamine.[52]

In November 2000, *The Vancouver Province* reported that two couriers employed by a heroin trafficking family living in Canada were sentenced in Hong Kong for laundering $35 million in drug money. Also in custody in Hong Kong is Helen Tan Jian-ping, who lived in Richmond County, British Columbia, and was, according to an Asian organized crime investigator in Ottawa, in charge of running the family's finances. Vancouver police files indicated that Helen Tan's husband was wanted in Canada and was believed to be hiding in China. According to the article, the syndicate to which Helen Tan is linked is one of the top 10 groups in the world, with possible links to the Big Circle Boys. The groups routinely used couriers to transport the proceeds of their narcotics sales to Hong Kong for laundering.[53]

Breaking the pattern of traditional organized crime groups, the major Chinese crime groups do not seek monopolies on drug trafficking activities or illicit financial transactions. Rather, members, especially those located in mainland China, play their most important role in brokering deals and facilitating the shipment of illegal contraband through Hong Kong to destinations abroad.[54]

Trafficking of Women

Background

Trafficking of persons, both for sexual exploitation and labor, is the fastest growing form of organized crime. It has been increasing dramatically in Canada, aided by the ruling of Human Resources and Development Canada in April 1998, that foreign nationals employed as "exotic dancers" were not displacing Canadian workers. This ruling created a legal avenue that was quickly exploited for illegal activities.[55] Trafficking became illegal only in 2001 after the

---

[52] Royal Canadian Mounted Police, Criminal Intelligence Program. "Drug Situation in Canada – 2001." (Ottawa 2002). <http://www.rcmp-grc.gc.ca>

[53] Fabian Dawson, "Drug Couriers Linked to Vancouver Jail," *The Vancouver Province*, November 10, 2002.

[54] "Asian Organized Crime," *International Crime Threat Assessment*, 2000. <http://www.fas.org/irp/threat/pub45270chap3.html#r14>

[55] Susan McClelland, "Inside the Sex Trade: Trafficking in Foreign Prostitutes Is One of the Fastest-Growing Illicit Activities in the World. Welcome to a Hidden Canada—and Lives of Quiet Desperation," *Maclean's* [Toronto], December 3, 2001. (Library of Congress InfoTrac OneFile)

passage of the 2001 Immigration Act; prostitution, however, remains legal in Canada.[56] Traffickers subsequently have found ways to exploit the system to provide sexual services. For example, foreign women can enter Canada legally as students, visitors, domestic workers, or mail-order brides.[57]

Human traffickers also make use of the Chinese smuggling network, known as "snakeheads," which often moves aliens into the United States in maritime vessels. Some gangs charge immigrants as much as US$40,000 for passage to the United States. The United States government estimates that 30,000 to 40,000 Chinese were smuggled into the United States in 1999, although reliable estimates of the number of Chinese who enter through Canada are not available through open-source materials.[58] Canadian officials currently estimate that more than 50 immigrant-smuggling groups are in Toronto alone.[59]

Human smuggling operations in Canada, whether confined to that country or intending to transport persons to the United States, are as varied as other illicit activities conducted by Asian organized crime groups. They may involve significant resources and the assistance of a well-established triad such as 14K, or they may be the work of a few individuals with no connections to well-known organized crime groups but having the proper connections to engage in human trafficking. Generally, trafficking networks reportedly are loose alliances among various groups that join forces to take advantage of existing opportunities. The success of the business is the primary motivating factor, and the triads do not hold a monopoly on the industry.[60]

The trafficking enterprises, however, usually are well structured. Responsibilities such as recruitment, document forgery, transport, and employment are subcontracted out.[61] For example, a woman in one of the countries typically involved in trafficking may respond to an advertisement for a seemingly legitimate job, only to be deceived into agreeing to be transported

---

[56] United States Department of State, *Country Reports on Human Rights Practices, 2002* (Washington: 2001). <http://www.state.gov>

[57] Lynn McDonald, *Migrant Sex Workers from Eastern Europe and the Former Soviet Union: The Canadian Case* (Toronto: Center for Applied Social Research, University of Toronto), November 2000. <http://www.swc-cfc.gc.ca/pubs/0662653351/index_e.html> and United States Department of State. *Country Reports on Human Rights Practices, 2001* (Washington: 2001). <http://www.state.gov>

[58] "Asian Organized Crime," *International Crime Threat Assessment*, 2000. <http://www.fas.org/irp/threat/pub45270chap2.html#r14>

[59] Susan Martin, "Dreams Ending in Nightmares," *Newsday*, March 11, 2001.

[60] Amy O'Neill Richard, *International Trafficking in Women to the United States: A Contemporary Manifestation of Slavery and Organized Crime* (Center for the Study of Intelligence), November 1999: 13.

[61] Ibid.

to Canada.[62] The groups engaged in trafficking often are involved in other related criminal activities.[63] INS raids on brothels operating in Toronto have uncovered the involvement of groups trafficking in heroin and counterfeiting. To date, it is unclear whether the more organized crime syndicates are the predominant traffickers of Asian women to the United States, although it is believed that they are not.[64]

The coercive tactics of trafficking groups continue to make themselves apparent. Women, often deceived or enticed with false promises to travel abroad and be employed in legitimate enterprises, may have their travel documents taken from them upon arrival in Canada. They also may be threatened, raped, or beaten if they protest their treatment. Another practice is to simply kidnap women off the streets of their home towns. Asian organized crime groups engaged in trafficking routinely make use of Asian street gangs as the muscle behind their operations, employing them as guards of the crime groups' "prisoners." [65]

Asian organized crime groups use a number of approaches to facilitate their trafficking operations. For example, they make frequent use of fake travel documents, often by recycling previously valid passports with legitimate visas and then making the necessary alterations by incorporating the recruit's picture, or trying to pass off the recruit as the person represented by the travel documents. As a way of saving money, they also have used Asian travel agencies that fail to verify all their visa applications.[66] Asian organized crime groups also use the technique of having a person, known as a "jockey," accompany a woman on a flight from Asia in order to lend legitimacy to her travel.[67] Still another common practice is for passengers on a flight destined for Canada to leave the airport and miss the remaining part of their flight when making a stopover in the United States. Canada's visa waiver program, unlike that of the United States, includes women originating in South Korea, providing a useful loophole.[68]

Profits from trafficking of women are remarkably high. Smugglers may receive between US$5,000 and US$15,000 for every person successfully smuggled into the United States, be that

---

[62] McClelland.
[63] Richard, 1.
[64] Lora Jo Woo, *Asian American Women: Issues, Concerns, and Responsive Human and Civil Rights Advocacy* (New York: Ford Foundation), 2002. <http://www.fordfound.org/publications/recent_articles/asian_american_women.cfm>
[65] Congressional Research Service, CRS Report for Congress. *Trafficking in Women and Children: The U.S. and International Response*, March 18, 2002. <http://fpc.state.gov/documents/organization/9107.pdf>
[66] Richard, 7.
[67] Richard, 8.
[68] Richard, 7.

person a woman or a minor. This fee includes payment for travel documents, the recruiting agents, and payment for the use of a "jockey" if one was used. Trafficked women subsequently are required to pay back their debt to the brothel in which they work; often the debt is as much as US$50,000. Chinese trafficking groups in Malaysia reportedly receive US$5,000 to US$7,000 for each Malaysian woman successfully delivered to the United States.[69] This industry may provide annual revenues of several million dollars to smugglers.

In the past, the Canadian system was unsuccessful in providing a real deterrence to those individuals or groups engaged in trafficking of persons. In many cases, the Criminal Code did not provide for harsh jail sentences for traffickers, and fines were often the only punishment available. Considering that the sex trade is so lucrative, most traffickers were willing to take the risk. In 2000, the federal government amended the Immigration Act to include fines up to CDN$1,000,000 and the possibility of life imprisonment for someone convicted of trafficking activities.[70]

The control that traffickers exercise over the persons they traffic also mitigates against effective deterrence. In Canada, trafficked women are generally required to testify against their employers in order for the latter to be convicted. However, cooperation with Canadian or U.S. authorities may expose the individuals or their families to great harm at the hands of the organized crime group in their native country. Because victims fear such reprisal, and hence refuse to testify, many criminals have been successful at avoiding jail time. This type of case was documented in October 2001 when law enforcement uncovered a prostitution ring that was transporting women from Malaysia to Vancouver. After their arrest, none of the eleven women involved would testify against their employers.[71]

Trafficking Operations Between 1999 and 2002

In February 2001, a raid of 20 brothels in San Francisco and Los Angeles uncovered a sex slave ring run by Asian organized crime gangs. According to Matthew Jacobs of the United States Attorney's Office, the investigation began in Toronto, which is believed to have been the transit point between Malaysia, Thailand, and Laos, and the eventual sale and transferal of women to brothels in California, using fake documents. Investigators determined that a number

---

[69] Richard, 20.
[70] McClelland, 4.
[71] McClelland, 4.

of the prostitutes detained had been arrested in September 1997 during RCMP raids of Canadian brothels. It is believed that many of the women were transferred regularly to different brothels around the United States and Canada as a way to avoid detection and bring customers new women.[72]

In March 2001, the RCMP infiltrated a prostitution ring estimated to have earned millions of dollars in illicit profits. Based in Ontario, the ring had succeeded in smuggling around 280 Korean women to Michigan on boats via the St. Clair River in Sarnia in just over a four-month period. Smuggling rings often use the St. Clair River for transport of illegal migrants as well. From Michigan, the women were moved to various locations, including massage parlors in various American cities, such as New York and Los Angeles. Investigators estimated that this ring, which had been in operation since the early 1990s, had moved as many as 1,200 Korean and Chinese women and immigrants who had been smuggled into the United States in 2000. Many of the women were under the age of 20.[73]

Financial Crimes

Major financial crimes tied to Chinese organized crime groups include credit card forgery, software technology piracy, and other high-tech crimes. The groups also pursue more traditional crimes such as vehicle theft, money laundering, and gun running. The Organized Crime Agency of British Columbia (OCABC) has singled out Asian organized crime groups as leaders in the counterfeit credit card business throughout North America. The Lower Mainland of British Columbia has experienced a disproportional outbreak of these crimes.[74]

Since 1999, credit card fraud has remained at extremely high levels in Canada, although there has been a recent decline. According to the CISC 2001 report, the total loss figure in 1999 was CDN$226.7 million and in 2000 it was CDN$172.5 million. In 1999, the value of forged credit card activity was CDN$123.6m; in 2000 it was CDN$81.1m; and in 2001 it was CDN$182.7m. The CISC report obtains its data from the Payment Card Partners, which represents the collective interests of Visa International, MasterCard, and American Express in

---

[72] Tom Godfrey, "Hookers Pipeline Through Canada to the U.S.," *The Toronto Sun*, February 17, 2001.
[73] McClelland, 3.
[74] Organized Crime Agency of British Columbia. *Annual Report – 2001.* < http://www.ocabc.org/>

Canada. Asian organized crime groups have worked with East European, East Indian, and Nigerian-based organized crime groups in this counterfeit card industry.[75]

Although South America and Mexico are emerging as centers for producing counterfeit credit cards in the Western Hemisphere, ethnic Chinese crime groups with operations in major commercial centers in East Asia, particularly Hong Kong and North America, are most often identified with fraudulent credit card activity. In 1999, police raided a counterfeit credit card manufacturing syndicate in southern China; the raid resulted in the seizure of thousands of fraudulent cards, uncut blank credit cards, magnetic strips, issuer holograms, encoders, laptop computers, and extensive manufacturing equipment. Investigations revealed that the scheme stretched to Hong Kong, Macau, Taiwan, Bangkok, Canada, Honolulu, and Buffalo, N.Y.[76]

On January 12, 2001, Canadian authorities uncovered one of the largest counterfeit credit card operations in Canadian history. Police located an "entire operational credit card factory," which had been in operation in Vancouver residences since 1994, and had the potential for fraud estimated at over CDN$200 million dollars.[77] Surplus counterfeiting equipment located at the "factory" would have potentially produced over CDN$1 billion worth of counterfeit credit cards. Authorities determined that equipment for the factory had been brought in from California, and that information "skimmed" from legitimate credit cards was being transferred to Vancouver by fax and subsequently sold to the counterfeit credit card factory. Twelve people with connections to the Big Circle Boys subsequently were charged with multiple offenses. The technique of skimming has become widespread in recent years.[78]

Asian organized crime groups in Calgary and elsewhere in Alberta also are involved in the production and distribution of counterfeit credit cards via networks throughout North America. In early 2002, a 15-month operation disrupted a huge Asian-based counterfeit credit card ring with connections in 34 countries. Eight counterfeit card factories were identified in Toronto, Calgary, Edmonton, and Vancouver. Authorities determined that the Big Circle Boys

---

[75] Criminal Intelligence Service Canada, *Annual Report on Organized Crime Canada* (Ottawa: 2002). <http://www.cics.gc.ca>
[76] "Asian Organized Crime," *International Crime Threat Assessment*, 2000. <http://www.fas.org/irp/threat/pub45270index html>
[77] Organized Crime Agency of British Columbia. Press Release, *1.5 Million Dollars in Counterfeit Credit Cards Recovered*, January 25, 2001. <http://www.ocabc.org/>
[78] "Twelve People Charged in Major Fake Credit Card, Drug Smuggling Ring," *Canadian Press Newswire*, July 3, 2002. (LexisNexis Document)

was involved in the Toronto portion of the operation.[79] A December 2002 article in *The Vancouver Sun* describes the police crackdown on an international crime ring that operated three credit card factories in the Lower Mainland of British Columbia for upwards of 10 years. The group had enough material in the factories to commit over CDN$200 million in fraud. Electronic data were stolen from legitimate credit cards at 116 retail outlets in North America. Fake cards then were sold around the world for between CDN$400 and CDN$800 each. The crime ring solicited the help of employees in gas stations, retail outfits, and restaurants, paying CDN$20 to CDN$40 for each card they scanned unnoticed by the cardholders, in palm-sized scanners. The supposed mastermind of the operation was Peter Liu, a Canadian citizen born in China. Reportedly, evidence established a connection between the Vancouver base of the crime ring and a member of the Big Circle Boys, who was sentenced in October 2002 for trafficking in counterfeit credit cards.[80]

Large-scale manufacture and distribution of pirated software, CDs, and DVDs are also common financial crimes that continue to affect U.S. businesses. In January 2002, the largest seizure of counterfeit DVDs in Canadian history took place in Vancouver. Police seized 6,700 DVDs at two locations in Chinatown. The estimated value of the items seized was approximately CDN$125,000. The DVDs were manufactured in Asia and then shipped to North America for sale.[81]

Chinese Organized Crime Groups Operating in Canada

Big Circle Boys

The Big Circle Boys had its origins in Guangzhou, the capital of Guangdong province, in the late 1960s. Its presence was detected in Canada in the late 1980s, and by the early 1990s it had established criminal cells throughout Canada where it has come to dominate the heroin trade within the country. Although not a traditional triad group, Big Circle includes substantial numbers of triad members and has secret membership rites.[82] The gang has cells active

---

[79] "Police Say Calgary Headquarters of Counterfeit Credit Card Operation, *Canadian Press Newswire*, January 31, 2002. (LexisNexis Document)

[80] Linda Slobodian, "Card Fraudsters Ripping off Banks for 10 Years," *The Vancouver Province*, December 13, 2002, A3. (Lexis Nexis Document)

[81] "Counterfeit DVD Seizure Sets Record: The 5,000 Fakes Nabbed in Raids on Two Vancouver Stores are Worth as Much as $125,000," *The Vancouver Sun*, February 2, 2002.

[82] Huston, 108-109.

worldwide, especially in Hong Kong and New York, and operates more as a loosely associated group of gangs than a centrally led organization. [83] The gang also makes use of sophisticated technologies such as counterfeiting machines to evade law enforcement investigations and is currently the most active Chinese organized crime group operating in Canada. The Big Circle Boys' greatest concentration is in Toronto.[84]

By the late 1990s, the group had approximately 500 members in Toronto and 250 in Vancouver.[85] Ex-mainland Chinese criminals comprise much of the organization. Following the pattern of most Asian organized crime groups, Big Circle has been known to cooperate with Vietnamese gangs and Laotian, Fukienese, and Taiwanese criminals, as well as non-Asian groups, such as the Italian mafia and the Hells Angels. The group essentially cooperates with any criminal organization able to facilitate its activities.[86]

The Big Circle Gang is primarily responsible for much of the exportation of Southeast Asian heroin that enters the United States, although its members also have been involved in the trafficking of other illegal narcotics, including South American cocaine and marijuana produced in Canada. They are known to work especially closely with Vietnamese gangs in drug trafficking.[87]

In addition to involvement in the heroin trade and other narcotics, the gang is extensively involved in alien smuggling, prostitution, gaming offenses, vehicle theft and trafficking, and various financial, intellectual property rights, and high-tech crimes. Big Circle has been connected to sex slave rings based in the United States that had apparent links to such activities in Toronto. Big Circle also have been linked to other groups that engaged in the trafficking of women. In regard to credit cards fraud, most open-source information suggests that the gang is responsible for a relatively high percentage of the counterfeit cards used in North America.[88] The group's members have established cells in New York, Boston, Seattle, San Francisco, and

---

[83] Jennifer Bolz, "Chinese Organized Crime and Illegal Alien Trafficking: Humans as a Commodity, *Asian Affairs, an American Review*, 22, no. 3 (1995). <http://www.csuohio.edu/polisci/courses/PSC422/Chinesecrime.htm>
[84] "Asian Organized Crime," *International Crime Threat Assessment*, 2000. <http://www.fas.org/irp/threat/pub45270chap3.html#r14>
[85] Mark Heinzl, "Organized Crime Begins Using Canada as a Base for Operations Ranging From Drugs to Car Theft," *Wall Street Journal*, July 6, 1998, A12.
[86] Bill Wallace, "Chinese Crime Ring Muscles In," *San Francisco Chronicle*, December 1, 1997.
[87] Nathanson Centre for the Study of Organized Crime and Corruption, *"A Quarterly Summary, January to March 2002"* [Toronto]. Website: <http://www.yorku.ca/nathanson/>
[88] Criminal Intelligence Service Canada. *Annual Report on Organized Crime Canada* (Ottawa: 2002). <http://www.cics.gc.ca>

Los Angeles. The gang was first identified in California in the early 1990s, when investigators uncovered a sophisticated high-tech counterfeit credit card operation supplying hundreds of credit cards. Police in San Francisco believe that the gang also is involved in the bootlegging of microchips and computer software, as well as prostitution and fraud in cooperation with the United Bamboo gang, the Four Seas Triad, and the Wah Ching.[89] In the city of Regina, the capital of the province of Saskatchewan, local individuals with links to the Big Circle Boys in Vancouver have been actively involved in counterfeiting, drug trafficking, and auto theft.[90]

United Bamboo Gang

The United Bamboo Gang (UBG) was established in Taiwan by ethnic Chinese individuals following World War II, and after the Kuomingtang party fled mainland China to avoid the communist takeover. It is currently the largest Taiwanese-based triad, with an estimated membership of 20,000. The group maintains criminal relationships with less organized gangs, including the Black Dragons, the Vietnamese V-Boys, and Hung Pho. In Canada, the group is believed to be involved in heroin trafficking and alien smuggling, which likely involves the trafficking of women as well. It is believed the gang is active in several U.S. cities, including Chicago, Honolulu, Houston, Miami, Phoenix, and various California cities. The UBG has built up a sophisticated network capable of supplying members with guns, narcotics, and fraudulent identifications.[91]

The alleged leader of the UBG is Chang An-lo, who has been one of the most wanted men in Taiwan for the past four years. He lives in China, apparently without fear of being extradited to Taiwan. It has been suggested that Chang might have government support because he advocates reunification of China and Taiwan. Chinese authorities, however, have claimed that they merely lack the evidence to prosecute him.[92] Another official has said that the issue is one of *guanxia*, meaning that Chang has connections with authorities in China who guarantee his safety. Chang's connections in China have raised the issue of possible collusion between organized crime figures and the Communist Party. The investigation of several high-ranking

---

[89] Wallace.
[90] Criminal Intelligence Service Canada. *Annual Report on Organized Crime Canada* (Ottawa: 2001). <http://www.cics.gc.ca>
[91] Kirsten Lindberg, "Emerging Organized Crime in Chicago," *International Review of Law, Computers & Technology*, July 1998.
[92] John Pomfret, "Made Man in China Has Gangland Ties, Party Pals," *Seattle Times*, January 21, 2001, A16.

communist officials in 2000 supports this suggestion. The mayor of Shenyang, a major city in northeastern China, was under investigation because of supposed links with the triads, but his case was subsequently dismissed. Shenyang's deputy, Ma Xiangdong, however, was arrested on bribery and smuggling charges.[93]

14K

The 14K, formed after the Second World War by Nationalists fleeing Communist China, is one of the most powerful triad organizations in Hong Kong, with over 30 sub-groups, more than 20,000 members, and a well-dispersed leadership.[94] The triad maintains a chapter in Toronto, and operates from New York and other U.S. cities.[95] Individual chapters operate autonomously. At times, this independence has led to competition and turf wars among chapters.[96]

14K is currently the fastest-growing triad in Canada. Prominent members have emigrated from Hong Kong and Macau to Canada. 14K's global network has allowed it to steal credit card data from all over the world, including the United States and Canada, by installing magnetic recorders in credit card terminals. Criminal investigations have determined that the group has had dealings with other Asian organized crime groups in New York and other U.S. cities.

14K activities appear to be expanding in Japan and Thailand, especially in connection with the trafficking of women into Japan.[97] Credit card forgery is also an expanding and very profitable activity for 14K in Canada and elsewhere.

Additional Groups

Several other Chinese triads and gangs are involved in criminal activities that affect both U.S. and Canadian interests. Open-source information provides little relevant data on these individual groups, however.

---

[93] Ibid.

[94] John Arquilla, *In Athena's Camp: Preparing for Conflict in the Information Age*, RAND, MR-880-OSD/RGI, 1997: 324.

[95] August Gribbin, "Global Crime Syndicates Target U.S. From Canada," *Insights on the News*, February 19, 2001.

[96] Arquilla, 324.

[97] The Protection Project. *A Human Rights Report on Trafficking of Persons, Especially Women and Children* (Washington, D.C.: 2002). < http://www.protectionproject.org/>

Kung Lok

The Kung Lok triad was founded in Toronto by Lau Wing Kui and has approximately 450 members in Canada as well as a number of connections in the United States.[98] According to a March 2000 article in the *Manila Standard*, the RCMP has identified Stanley Ho, a Macau gambling tycoon active in Canada and linked to several illegal activities, as having links to Kung Lok.[99] A man identified as Sonny Kwan, an associate of a former Kung Lok leader, was one of three men arrested in December 2002 following the kidnapping of a daughter of a Hong Kong businessman and her boyfriend.[100]

Sun Yee On

Members of the Sun Yee On triad have settled in Toronto, Edmonton, and Vancouver, although they are active in Alberta and British Columbia as well.[101] They are involved in the trafficking of heroin and methamphetamines, as well as alien smuggling, credit card fraud, and trafficking of women to the United States. The triad appears to have ties to New York's Tung On gang.[102] Evidence suggests that Sun Yee On is involved with independent smuggling operations to traffic women and is becoming increasingly active in Japan in the furtherance of this activity.[103] Members of the triad exhibit a strong group identity, exhibit great caution in admitting new members, and adhere to a relatively strict command and control structure in comparison to other triads.[104]

Wah Ching Gang

The Wah Ching Gang, which originated in California, has engaged in the smuggling and trafficking of Asian women; it is also is involved in gambling, robbery, murder, drug trafficking, and loan sharking. The gang has connections to other Asian organized crime groups in Boston,

---

[98] Bolz.

[99] "PNP Hit for Slow Probe of Ho," *Manila Standard* [Manila], March 22, 2000. (Lexis Nexis document)

[100] Rob Lamberti, "Accused Linked to Asian Gangster," *The Toronto Sun*, January 1, 2003.

[101] "Asian Organized Crime," *International Crime Threat Assessment*, 2000. <http://www.fas.org/>

[102] Ibid.

[103] The Protection Project. *A Human Rights Report on Trafficking of Persons, Especially Women and Children* (Washington, D.C.: 2002). < http://www.protectionproject.org/>

[104] "Asian Organized Crime," *International Crime Threat Assessment*, 2000. <http://www.fas.org/>

Dallas, Los Angeles, New York City, Seattle, Toronto, and Vancouver. The Wah Ching is known to employ Asian street gangs such as the Black Dragons and Koolboyz for protection at brothels.[105]

Wo Group

The Wo Group has 10 sub-groups and approximately 20,000 members worldwide.[106] Little specific information is available on the Wo Group's activities in the United States and Canada. It is known, however, that the Wo Hop To sub-group is involved in both heroin trafficking and alien smuggling in the United States. The leader of the Wo Hop To is Peter Chong; it is believed that the group has undergone significant expansion on the West Coast, and in San Francisco in particular.[107]

Vietnamese-Based Criminal Groups

Vietnamese criminal groups range from street gangs engaged in drug trafficking to highly sophisticated groups. The groups are known to be very violent, and some members are reported to have been trained in the use of weapons and explosives. The groups are expanding in the area of high technology crimes and have engaged in the theft of computer parts, which they sell on the black market to third world countries. Vietnamese groups also are believed to be involved in the trafficking of women.

Vietnamese groups, especially the street gangs, are generally less formal in structure than many other organized crime groups. This lack of organization often has meant that they are extremely mobile and able to cooperate with other organizations. Quite often, Vietnamese groups lack ties to any one community and, therefore, may travel to various cities to set up temporary operations. These networking activities have led to fear that they eventually will organize into more formal and structured groups.[108]

Vietnamese organized crime groups also are known to work with the Hells Angels, mainly in British Columbia, for the large-scale cultivation and exportation of marijuana. These activities have been expanding eastward across Canada to Ontario. It is estimated that there are

---

[105] Richard, 14.
[106] Bolz.
[107] Nikos Passas, *Transnational Crime* (Dartmouth: Ashgate, 1999), 82.
[108] Lindberg.

approximately 15,000 to 20,000 marijuana-growing operations in the Lower Mainland with an estimated sale value of CDN$6 billion.[109]

Current estimates in British Columbia are that Vietnamese crime groups, in concert with their Hells Angels counterparts, control roughly 85 percent of marijuana production and distribution in the region.[110] CISC reports that Chinese organized crime groups have purchased marijuana from Vietnamese groups with the intent of transporting it to the United States for sale. In January 2000, the Vancouver Police Department Gang Crime Unit of the Organized Crime Agency of British Columbia (OCABC) began an investigation known as Project Coconut regarding the involvement of members of the Big Circle Boys in a major counterfeit credit card fraud scheme.[111] Upon investigation, police discovered that the suspects also were allegedly smuggling significant amounts of marijuana into the state of Washington by boat from a marina on Vancouver Island. In this particular operation, Vietnamese marijuana producers were providing marijuana to Chinese exporters, who then arranged for transport by ship and delivery to distributors in Bellingham and Seattle, WA. Interdiction efforts resulted in the interception and seizure of shipments totaling approximately 555 pounds of marijuana.[112]

Interdiction efforts in January, February, and June 2001 by OCABC in Vancouver and Richmond again resulted in significant seizures. In the raids, police seized 825 pounds of British Columbia marijuana valued at approximately US$2m, 3,000 ecstasy pills, and U.S. and Canadian currency valued at approximately CDN$300,000.[113] In another raid, using information obtained from the Project Coconut investigation, Canadian Customs Inspectors at the Pacific Highway commercial truck border crossing seized 49.5 kilos of cocaine and a large sum of U.S. cash that had been hidden in the sleeping compartment of a tractor-trailer entering Canada.[114]

In January 2002, police across Canada initiated Operation Green Sweep, a cross-country crackdown on hydroponics labs used for the cultivation of marijuana plants. The operation resulted in the seizure of 47,000 plants estimated to be worth approximately CDN$47 million.

---

[109] Criminal Intelligence Service Canada. *Annual Report on Organized Crime Canada* (Ottawa: 2002). <http://www.cics.gc.ca>
[110] Ibid.
[111] Organized Crime Agency of British Columbia, Press Release, *Counterfeiting of Credit Cards and the Smuggling of Hundreds of Pounds of Marijuana into the United States Halted*, July 3, 2002. <http://www.ocabc.org/>
[112] Ibid.
[113] Ibid.
[114] Ibid.

One hundred thirty-six people, mostly of Vietnamese origin, were arrested in connection with the operation. The majority of the seizures took place in Ontario.[115]

According to a CISC report, Vietnamese groups control approximately 80 to 85 percent of the heroin trade in the Kamloops area of British Columbia. Vancouver also is used as a trans-shipment center for trafficking heroin into the United States, and is reported to have approximately 10,000 marijuana growing operations. Vietnamese gangs are reputed to be controlling much of this activity.[116] Vietnamese crime groups import heroin directly from the Golden Triangle region, almost always through Vietnam or China. Typically, couriers bring in body packs that contain less than five kilograms per person per trip.[117]

The West Coast Players

The Immigration and Naturalization Service has discovered a Canadian group in Canada, called the West Coast Players that has ties to Asian organized crime groups in British Columbia.[118] According to an article in *The Vancouver Sun*, the group recruits underage girls in the Lower Mainland of British Columbia and traffics them to the United States, and Los Angeles in particular, to work as prostitutes.[119] The group supposedly is also active in the city of Coquitlam, British Columbia.

FOREIGN TERRORIST ORGANIZATIONS

Background

Canada's geographic proximity to the United States, together with the comparative ease of entering into the country, makes it a prime locale for terrorist organizations. According to a Canadian Security Intelligence Service report in 2000, about 50 terrorist groups, with more than 350 members, were using Canada as a base from which to conduct their activities.[120] Although

---

[115] Brett Clarkson, "Cops Go for the Green," *The Toronto Sun,* January 31, 2002.
[116] Criminal Intelligence Service Canada. *Annual Report on Organized Crime Canada* (Ottawa: 2001).
<http://www.cics.gc.ca>
[117] "Government Reports on Vietnamese, Chinese Crime Gangs," *Paris AFP (North European Service) in English,* August 20, 1999 (FBIS Document FTS19990820001434).
[118] Richard, 21.
[119] Chris Nuttal-Smith, "B.C. Singled Out by CIA Report on Prostitution: Law Enforcement Officials Worry that Established Sex Trade Gangs are Making New Links to Organized Crime," *The Vancouver Sun*, April 14, 2000.
[120] Canadian Security Intelligence Service, Report 2000/04. *International Terrorism: The Threat to Canada*, May 3, 2000. <http://www.csis-scrs.gc.ca/eng/miscdocs/200004_e.html>

many of these groups may have been using individuals only to conduct fund raising activities, it was feared that active cells might exist. The report noted that the scope of several of these organizations had changed from being involved in "support roles, such as fund-raising and [weapons] procurement, to actually planning and preparing terrorist acts" from Canada.[121]

The groups cited in the report included Hezbollah and other Shiite Islamic terrorist organizations; several Sunni Islamic extremist groups with ties to Egypt, Libya, Algeria, Lebanon, and Iran; the PKK; the Provisional IRA; the Tamil Tigers; and all of the major Sikh terrorist groups.[122]

In its 2001 *Anti-Terrorism Act*, the Canadian government officially bans 16 terrorist organizations from conducting any type of activities within the country and allows the government to designate specific individuals and groups as terrorist organizations. The Act also provides for rigid criminal penalties against these individuals or groups and the seizure of assets. This move has dealt a serious legal blow to groups that have relied on Canada as a financial resource. The list, however, still contains fewer than half of the groups listed on a similar list organized by the U.S. State Department. Included on the Canadian list are Al-Gama'a al-Islamiyya, al-Ittihad al-Islam, al-Qaeda, Algerian Armed Islamic Group, Asbat Al-Ansar, Aum Shinrikyo, Egyptian al-Jihad, Hamas, Harakat ul-Mujahedin, Hezbollah, Islamic Army of Aden, Jaish-e Mohammed, the Kurdistan Workers Party (PKK), Palestinian Islamic Jihad, Salifist Group for Call and Combat, and Vanguards of Conquest.[123]

Al-Qaeda

Research indicates that al-Qaeda operatives, more than any other group, have sought refuge in Canadian territory for the purpose of directing attacks against U.S. interests around the globe, thus continuing the strategy the group has implemented of developing networks both for financial and logistical reasons.[124] To date there is no indication that al-Qaeda has modified its goals in regard to targeting the United States, and CSIS has also stated its belief that there are

---

[121] Colin Nickerson, "Canada Gets Reputation as a Haven for Fugitives," *Boston Globe*, December 21, 2000, A1. <http://proquest.umi.com/pqdweb?Did=0000...Fmt=3&Deli=1&Mtd=1&Idx=2&Sid=15&RQT=309>
[122] Ibid.
[123] Stewart Bell, "Liberals Relent, Hezbollah Outlawed: Graham Says It's Due to Recent Evidence," *National Post* [Toronto], December 12, 2002, A1.
[124] Peter L. Bergen, "*Holy War, Inc.*" (New York: Touchstone, 2002), 200.

sleeper cells operating in Canada that are capable of providing support for terrorist activities in North America.[125] Several incidents since 1999 indicate an al-Qaeda presence in Canada.

One such incident concerned Abdel Ghani. Ghani was arrested by police in Brooklyn in 1999. Ghani's telephone number had been found in the pocket of Ahmed Ressam. When he was arrested while attempting to sneak into the United States from Canada, Ressam was an Algerian national and member of the Algerian Armed Islamic group. Information obtained from Ghani led police to Abdel Hakim Tizegha, an al-Qaeda member living in Canada. He was arrested on December 24, 1999, after having sneaked across the U.S. border near Blaine, Washington.[126]

Another case involved Nabil al-Marabh. In June 2001, al-Marabh, suspected by U.S. authorities of providing support to the September 11 hijackers, was caught as he tried to cross into the United States from Canada, using a fake Canadian passport. Despite having been denied refugee status and deported in 1994, al-Marabh had been able to re-enter Canada without difficulty in 2001. Al-Marabh had shared a residence and worked at the same company as Raed Hijazi, an alleged al-Qaeda operative. Al-Marabh allegedly transferred funds to bank accounts and made fake IDs for some of the September 11 hijackers.[127] After his capture in 2001, al-Marbh was ultimately released on bail, despite having been deported from Canada in 1994, and having known ties to al-Qaeda. The decision to release him was defended by Canada's Minister of Immigration after September 11 because the minister believed that to detain him without substantial evidence would be to violate Canada's policies. U.S. authorities took al-Marabh into custody on September 19, 2001, in a Chicago suburb, because of his alleged connection with the September 11 attacks.[128]

International attacks that have possible al-Qaeda connections also have roots in Canada. The April 11, 2002 bombing of a synagogue in Tunisia may be linked to al-Qaeda operatives who planned the attack while living in Canada and Germany, according to an article in the *Boston Globe*. Niser bin Muhammad Nasar Nawar, an Islamic radical connected to al-Qaeda, is suspected of planning the attack while living in Montreal. According to a French official, Nawar entered Montreal in 1999, possibly with the assistance of the Tunisian Fighting Group, an organization with ties to al-Qaeda and with followers in Canada, France, and Germany.

---

[125] Dana Priest, "Canadian 'Sleepers' in Contact With U.S. Cells," *Toronto Star*, December 26, 2002.
[126] Kenneth R. Timmerman, "Canadian Border Open to Terrorists," *Insight on the News* [Washington], December 17, 2001. (Library of Congress InfoTrac OneFile)
[127] Berlau.
[128] Ibid.

Although Canadian immigration officials have no record of Nawar entering the country and living in Montreal, these officials admit that they were unable to monitor scores of Tunisians who entered the country in 1999 and 2000 using fraudulent student visas.[129]

In yet another case, Bob Runciman, Ontario's Minister of Public Safety and Security, asserted that an al-Qaeda sleeper cell fled Ontario in May 2002, after coming under police investigation. Although officials determined that many of the subjects were not involved in any criminal activity, an undetermined number were not cleared of involvement in terrorist activity and were sought for questioning.[130]

In June 2002, an Algerian man named Amine Mezbar, who maintained his residence in Montreal, was sent to the Netherlands where Dutch prosecutors have alleged he was forging documents and assisting an al-Qaeda group in Europe in plans to blow up the U.S. Embassy in Paris. Dutch authorities sought Mezbar so that he could be charged, along with the six other men awaiting trial who are alleged to make up the European cell. Mezbar had at least three aliases and was living in Montreal at the time of his arrest.[131]

A December 2002 article in *The Ottawa Citizen* reported that the CSIS had accused Ahmed Khadr, a Canadian citizen, of having strong links with Mohammad Harkat, who in turn was connected with Abu Zubaydah, al-Qaeda's chief operational planner. Khadr also is suspected to have ties to Mahmoud Jaballah, a suspected member of al-Jihad. Khadr was last sighted in Afghanistan in November 2001.[132]

In 1995, Mohammad Harkat, who later was discovered to have links with al-Qaeda's chief operational planner, Abu Zubaydah, arrived in Canada using a forged Saudi passport and claiming he had been persecuted in Algeria. Despite being under investigation for terrorist activities since 1997, he gained refugee status, and his deportation hearing did not commence until January 2003. Harkat was purported to have connections with several violent Islamic extremist groups, including the Armed Islamic Group in Algeria as well as two Saudi charitable groups, the Muslim World League and the International Islamic Relief Organization. He is

---

[129] Nickerson.

[130] Bob Runciman, "Suspected Terrorist Cell Flees Ontario," *Buffalo News*, May 26, 2002, A9.

[131] CBC News, "Algerian Man Won't Fight Extradition to Netherlands," June 28 2002; and "Terrorist Suspect Consents to Extradition from Canada," June 27, 2002. < http://www.cbc.ca/>

[132] Andrew Duffy, "The Case Against Harkat: CSIS Is Sure the Ottawa Man Is an al-Qaeda Sleeper," December 21, 2002, B1. (Lexis Nexis Document)

suspected of assisting terrorists, including the September 11 hijackers.[133] According to CSIS documents, Harakat was believed to be a "sleeper," waiting for instructions and was in contact with suspected al-Qaeda operatives as recently as December 2002.[134]

A January 2002 article in the *The Vancouver Sun* claims that evidence uncovered from the Afghanistan residence of a man thought to be Osama bin Laden's military chief identifies two Canadian citizens as having links to al-Qaeda.[135] One of the men was identified as Al Rauf bin Al Habib Bin Yousef Al-Jiddi; he may be in the company of another man named Faker Boussora.

Algerian Armed Islamic Group (GIA)

In 1999, Algerian national Ahmed Ressam was arrested in Port Angeles, Washington, after U.S Customs agents stopped him during an attempt to smuggle bomb-making material into the United States from Canada. A member of the Algerian Armed Islamic group, which has strong ties to al-Qaeda, Ressam was planning to bomb Los Angeles International Airport with the explosives he was smuggling into the United States.[136] Ressam was trained at bin Laden's Khalden camp in Afghanistan.[137] Upon his return to Canada, he traveled to Vancouver and spent a number of days in a motel room assembling explosives with Abdelmajid Dahoumane, an accomplice arrested in Algeria about a year later.[138]

Ressam had lived in Canada since entering on a false passport number in 1994. He used a fake baptismal certificate to receive an authentic passport, which he used when trying to enter the United States.[139] In addition, Ressam was reported to have been linked with Abu Zubaydah, al-Qaeda's chief operational planner and close associate of bin Laden until his arrest in Pakistan in 2002.[140]

---

[133] Ibid.

[134] Dana Priest, "Canadians Hunt al-Qaeda Loyalists," *Milwaukee Journal Sentinel*, December 26, 2002.

[135] "Turks Nab 3 Suspected of Plotting Attack in Israel," *The Vancouver Sun*, February 20, 2002. A12.

[136] Stinson.

[137] "Asian Organized Crime," *International Crime Threat Assessment*, 2000.
<http://www.fas.org/irp/threat/pub45270chap3.html#r14>

[138] John Geddes, "The Terrorists Next Door," *Maclean's* (Toronto), September 24, 2001. (Library of Congress InfoTrac OneFile)

[139] "Guns and Grenades," *Canada and the World Backgrounder* [Ontario], December 2002. (Library of Congress InfoTrac OneFile)

[140] Bergen, 143.

Although the CSIS had a 400-page file on Ressam and Italian and French intelligence agencies had reported his associates' activities, this information reportedly was not shared with Montreal police or Canadian immigration officials. In 2001, one of Ressam's associates, Fateh Kamel, the alleged GIA leader in Montreal, was put on trial in France for a bomb plot against the Paris subway.[141] Kamel, who sought political asylum in Canada and held dual citizenship, admitted during the trial to connections with Ressam in Canada.[142]

In December 1999, another supposed accomplice of Ressam, Bouabide Chamchi, was arrested while trying to drive across the border into Vermont. Chamchi was eventually linked through a female companion to several men who had trained as terrorists in Afghanistan. According to an *Insight on the News* article, Chamchi was planning an attack to coincide with Ressam's.[143] It is unclear whether Chamchi is a member of the Algerian Armed Islamic Group.

Egyptian Al-Jihad

Members of the Egyptian Al-Jihad movement, which was responsible for terrorist attacks on Egyptian officials and western targets in Egypt until the mid-1990s, have been identified as living in Canada. Mahmoud Jaballah, an Egyptian-born resident of Toronto, is alleged to have links to both al-Jihad and al-Qaeda. In April 2003, Jalabad was denied his refugee claim by Canada's Immigration and Refugee Board, which found him to be complicit in crimes against humanity.[144] First arrested in 1999 for supposed ties to the Egyptian Islamic Jihad, he was arrested most recently in August 2001 at the request of the CSIS. Another man currently being held by Canadian authorities, identified as Mohamed Zeki Mahjoub, has been charged with having ties to Osama bin Laden and Jaballah. Egyptian authorities have identified Majoub as a member of the Vanguards of Conquest, a radical faction of the al-Jihad terrorist organization.[145]

---

[141] Hal Berton, "'Terrorist Tupperware Parties': CSIS watched the fledgling terrorist cell in Montreal, But Did Nothing About It," *The Vancouver Sun*, August 10, 2002.
[142] Verena Von Derschau, "Defendant: Apartment Was For Meetings," *Associated Press*, February 16, 2001.
[143] Timmerman.
[144] Peter Edwards, "Refugee Found Linked to Terrorism," *Toronto Star*, April 11, 2003, A14.
[145] Bill Schiller, "Egypt to Toronto: Al Jihad Casts Wide Net," *Toronto Star*, October 21, 2001, A1.

Hamas

Hamas has been active in Canada for a decade, using the country to derive a part of its financial and political support.[146] The *Anti-Terrorism Act* forbids Hamas from continuing its fundraising activities in Canada. No substantial reports indicate possible Hamas activities in Canada that could affect the United States.

Hezbollah

In 1997, CISC reported that Hezbollah, also known as the Islamic Jihad for the Liberation of Palestine, had established a base of operations in Canada with the purpose of assisting and supporting terrorists seeking a safe haven in North America. The group is believed to have undertaken major fundraising activities in Canada under the guise of charity drives for schools, hospitals, and other social services.[147] It is not yet known how the organization's representatives in Canada will adapt to the illegal status conferred on it by the *Anti-Terrorism Act* of 2001.

A February 2002 article in *The Ottawa Citizen* indicates that a Hezbollah cell based in Charlotte, North Carolina, had links to at least two operatives living in Vancouver. According to findings of the CSIS investigation in Vancouver, Said Harb, a Charlotte Internet startup company owner, purchased equipment for Hezbollah in Vancouver. In July 2000, Federal Bureau of Investigation agents arrested Harb.[148]

According to a December 2002 *National Post* article, which was based on a police report, a captured Hezbollah agent in Montreal has claimed that the group has agents in major cities throughout Canada and is collecting video footage for potential bomb sites in Canada. Group members in Quebec and Ontario also allegedly run active auto theft rings.[149] A 2002 report by the Nathanson Centre on Organized Crime in Canada seems to confirm the article's finding that Middle Eastern organized crime groups in Canada are using approximately 10 percent of the profits from auto-theft rings to fund the militant group Hezbollah.[150]

---

[146] Stewart Bell , "Liberals Ban Hamas, Five Others: But not Hezbollah," *National Post* [Toronto], November 28, 2002, A5. (Lexis Nexis Document).

[147] Lorraine Passchier , "Canada Shifts into Overdrive," *CTVNEWS* [Canada], October 15, 2002.

[148] Andrew Duffy, "CSIS spies to Testify at U.S. Trial: In North American First, Agents Will Give Evidence Against Alleged Terrorist," *The Ottawa Citizen*, February 7, 2002, A5.

[149] Stewart Bell, "Liberals Relent, Hezbollah Outlawed: Graham Says It's Due to Recent Evidence," *National Post* [Toronto], December 12, 2002, A1. (Lexis Nexis Document)

[150] Nathanson Centre for the Study of Organized Crime and Corruption.

A February 2003 *National Post* article details the activities of Mohamad Hammoud, the leader of a Hezbollah terrorist cell in Canada who was convicted in the United States. Hammoud also ran an intricate cigarette smuggling and credit card fraud ring in North Carolina that financed Hezbollah. U.S. officials believe that Imad Mugniyah, a senior Hezbollah leader with a US$25m reward on his head in the United States, is working with Hammoud's Canadian cell.[151]

The Kurdistan Workers Party (PKK)

The *National Post* quotes the CSIS as saying that the PKK had sent agents to Montreal throughout the 1990s to gain control over the Kurdish community there. The article also notes that the arrest of PKK leader Abdullah Ocalan in Kenya in 2000 sparked riots in Ottawa, indicating a strong support in the community for PKK activities.[152] With current uncertainty in Iraq regarding the Kurdish population, it is possible that the PKK could turn its sights on the United States if the party were not content with the political options available for that population in the coming months.

COOPERATION BETWEEN TERRORISTS AND ORGANIZED CRIME

Introduction

The international political and economic changes that drug-trafficking and organized crime groups exploit to facilitate their activities also enhance the ability of terrorist groups to operate worldwide. International terrorist groups are particularly adept at exploiting the advantages of more open borders and the globalization of international commerce to move people, money, and material across national borders. Like trafficking and other criminal organizations, terrorist groups are becoming more sophisticated in using computer technology to enhance their communications and logistics networks.

Although terrorist groups and criminal organizations have similar requirements for moving people, money, and material across international borders, traditionally there was minimal cooperation between them. Terrorist groups maintain their own clandestine networks and typically control all aspects of their operations to minimize the risk of infiltration and exposure.

---

[151] Stewart Bell, "Terrorist Plotted to Kill Prosecutor, U.S. Court Told Had Agents in Vancouver," *National Post* [Toronto], February 28, 2003.
[152] Bell.

However, the potential exists for greater interaction as transnational terrorist groups and criminal organizations pursue similar strategies along parallel lines, despite their disparate goals.

Drug Trafficking

Both organized crime and terrorist groups have used narcotics in order to generate revenues to support their activities. According to a confidential November 2001 RCMP report entitled *Narco-terrorism and Canada*, money generated from hashish trafficked into Canada has been used to finance terrorists. Approximately 100 tons of Southwest Asian hashish is brought into Canada every year, valued at roughly CDN$20m. The report deduces that a portion of this amount annually finances terrorist groups in Afghanistan and Pakistan because terrorists gain a portion of narcotics profits by taxing the producers.[153]

Although the report additionally states that Canadian law enforcement has not recently documented any "large-scale" importation of Southwest Asian heroin that originated in Afghanistan, there are concerns that this belies the actual situation. The UN Drug Control Program found that Afghanistan produced 3,300 tons of poppies used to make Opium in 2000. Estimates for 2001 are for only 185 tons because of the Taliban's ban on growing poppies; it is believed, however, that much of the crop has been stockpiled and that farmers are now reinitiating their efforts.[154] An article in the March/April 2003 *Turkistan Newsletter* supports the theory that Afghani farmers are expanding their cultivation of the poppy as well as setting up factories to produce heroin. Southwest Asian heroin from Pakistan and Afghanistan is mainly transported to Canada through Montreal and Toronto. [155]

Forged Documents

Terrorist and organized crime groups are also suspected of cooperating with each other to obtain forged documentation for identification and travel. In November 2001, police arrested a Hamilton, Ontario man suspected of supplying forged documents to Saeed Ahmed Alghamdi, one of the September 11 hijackers. The man arrested, Gideon Glen McGuire Augier, is a

---

[153] "Canadian Report Says Some of $20 Million Hashish Imports Financed Terrorism," *The Globe and Mail* [Toronto], July 15, 2002 (FBIS Document FTS20020715000129).
[154] Ibid.
[155] Sohail Abdul Nasir, "Americans Like to Think the War in Afghanistan Is Over, but That Would Be a Serious Mistake," *Turkistan Newsletter*, March/April 2003.

convicted fraud artist and suspected member of a forgery ring. The police reportedly examined documents in the name of Samen Singh that were possibly used by Alghamdi. Augier acknowledged dealing with Russian organized crime but denied any involvement with al-Qaeda. Police were actively exploring the possibility that one of Augier's regular contacts was a Russian organized crime figure with links to al-Qaeda who was assisting in the procurement of forged documents for the terrorist group.[156]

"Snakeheads" and other human traffickers are believed to be active in other criminal activities. Terrorist organizations could use these Chinese human smuggling syndicates to provide fake identity document services, although no evidence exists yet of such a trend.[157]

The Canadian Diamond Industry

With the discovery of vast resources of diamonds in Canada in 1991, the country has quickly become the world's fifth largest producer of diamonds. Once additional diamond mines are opened, Canada may become the world's second or third largest diamond producer. A *National Post* article in August 2002, which attributes its information to a criminal intelligence report by the CISC, warns that this emerging uncut diamond industry may be exploited by terrorist and organized crime groups seeking to finance ventures into illicit drugs, arms trafficking, and violence. Although no clear indication exists in the open literature of any criminal or terrorist infiltration of the industry, the article notes the huge potential for illicit activities that the burgeoning Canadian diamond trade represents, especially under cover of Canada's sterling reputation in the industry.[158] Taking the opposite position, an RCMP report notes that the chances of such exploitation are highly unlikely because BHP Billiton Diamonds, the company in charge of the country's only operational diamond mine in Canada, has put in place strict measures to ensure security at every stage of diamond processing.[159]

---

[156] Joan Walters, "Criminals Support Terrorists; Organized Crime Provides Forged ID," *Hamilton Spectator*, November 2, 2001.

[157] Paul J. Smith, "The Terrorists and Crime Bosses Behind the Fake Passport Trade," *Jane's Intelligence Review*, July 1, 2001.

[158] Adrian Humphreys, "Criminals May be Casing Canada's Diamond Trade," *National Post* [Toronto], August 24, 2002, A10.

[159] Royal Canadian Mounted Police, Criminal Intelligence Program. "Link Between Al-Qaeda and the Diamond Industry." Ottawa 2002. <http://www.rcmp-grc.gc.ca/crim_int/diamond_e htm>

CONCLUSION

The United States and Canada share a unique relationship based on democratic ideology and geographic proximity. These advantages have facilitated the development of a mutually beneficial partnership between the two countries in the form of international trade, relatively open borders, and integration between the two societies. Each country is the largest trading partner of the other. However, the very benefits stemming from this relationship continue to be exploited by both organized crime and terrorist groups.

Because of inadequate funding and insufficient personnel on both sides of the border, the U.S.-Canadian border remains relatively porous and can be crossed in many areas without fear of encountering security personnel. The sheer length of the U.S.-Canadian border, at over 5,500 miles and with vast zones of virtually nonexistent border demarcation, make it unlikely that any amount of funding can entirely address the border issue. Therefore, Canadian authorities should emphasize port security and immigration policy as a means of ensuring that Asian organized crime and terrorist groups cannot enter Canada in the first place. If port security is strengthened and immigration policy is tightened, the immense problem of border security will become a secondary issue.

Since September 11, Canada has devoted a great deal of attention to the issues of immigration and refugee policy, port security, and border security. The relatively short period of time since September 11 makes it unclear whether the initiatives undertaken will prove successful.

Ethnic Chinese triads, gangs, and syndicates have set up vast operations in Canada and constitute the greatest criminal threats in Canada. These Asian groups are involved in a wide variety of criminal activities, primarily in large population centers. Although virtually homogenous in makeup, Asian organized crime groups continue to deal with non-Asian groups in pursuit of profitable activities. No firm links have been established between Asian groups and terrorist activities based in Canada, however.

The extent to which Canada possesses terrorist sleeper cells capable of carrying out attacks against targets in North America remains uncertain. Research from 1999 onwards has uncovered numerous accounts of individuals who have links to terrorist organizations, and who may have been in the process of orchestrating terrorist attacks. However, increased security measures since September 11 have resulted in greater vigilance and a number of successful arrests over the past four years. With regard to complicity between terrorist and organized crime groups, there is consensus among various experts that both groups at times use the same methods and activities to achieve their revenue goals. However, specific details on these activities remain relatively elusive in open-source materials. Despite the differing motivational factors of these groups, it is possible that a greater complicity will evolve between them.

BIBLIOGRAPHY

Arquilla, John. *In Athena's Camp: Preparing for Conflict in the Information Age.* (MR-880-OSD/RGI) Washington: RAND, 1997.

"Asian Organized Crime," *International Crime Threat Assessment*, 2000. <http://www.fas.org/irp/threat/pub45270chap3.html#r14>

Baxter, James. "Current Senate Report Said to Confirm 1996 Warnings on Canadian Port Security," *National Post* [Toronto], March 19, 2002 (FBIS Document EUP 20020319000054).

Bell, Stewart. "Liberals Ban Hamas, Five Others: But not Hezbollah," *National Post* [Toronto], November 28, 2002, A5.

Bell, Stewart. "Liberals Relent, Hezbollah Outlawed: Graham Says It's Due to Recent Evidence," *National Post* [Toronto], December 12, 2002, A1.

Bell, Stewart. "Terrorist Plotted to Kill Prosecutor, U.S. Court Told Had Agents in Vancouver," *National Post* [Toronto], February 28, 2003, A2.

Bergen, Peter L. *"Holy War, Inc,"* New York: Touchstone, 2002: 143, 200.

Berlau, John. "Canada Turns into Terrorist Haven," *Insight on the News*, June 24, 2002. <http://www.insightmag.com/news/254290.html>

Berry, LaVerle. *Russian Organized Crime and the Global Narcotics Trade.* Washington: Library of Congress, Federal Research Division, March 2002.

Berton, Hal. "'Terrorist Tupperware Parties': CSIS Watched the Fledgling Terrorist Cell in Montreal, But Did Nothing About It," *The Vancouver Sun*, August 10, 2002.

Bolz, Jennifer. "Chinese Organized Crime and Illegal Alien Trafficking: Humans as a Commodity," *Asian Affairs, an American Review*, 22, no. 3 (1995).

Brzezinski, Matthew. "Re-engineering the Drug Business," *New York Times*, June 23, 2002.

Canadian Embassy, *"Canada's Actions Against Terrorism Since September 11th."* Washington: 2003. < http://www.canadianembassy.org/border/backgrounder-en.asp>

"Canadian Police: Huge Heroin Deals Funded From Hong Kong," *Hong Kong South China Sunday Morning Post in English* [Honk Kong], June 27, 1999 (FBIS Document CPP19990628000046).

"Canadian Report Says Some of $20 Million Hashish Imports Financed Terrorism," *The Globe and Mail* [Toronto], July 15, 2002 (FBIS Document FTS20020715000129).

Canadian Security Intelligence Service. *International Terrorism: The Threat to Canada.* Report No. 2000/04, May 3, 2000. <http://www.csisscrs.gc.ca/eng/miscdocs/200004_e.html>

CBC News, "Algerian Man Won't Fight Extradition to Netherlands," June 28, 2002; and "Terrorist Suspect Consents to Extradition From Canada," June 27, 2002. < http://www.cbc.ca/>

CBC Ottawa, "CSIS Says Ottawa Pizza Driver Is al-Qaeda Sleeper Agent," December 17, 2002. <http://ottawa.cbc.ca/newsinreview/dec/dec17.html>

Chu, Yiu Kong. *The Triads as Business.* New York: St. Edmundsbury, 2000.

Clarkson, Brett. "Cops Go for the Green," *The Toronto Sun,* January 31, 2002.

Cohen, Tom. "Canada Denies Bail to Chinese Smuggler," *Pittsburgh Post*, December 6, 2000, A5.

"Counterfeit DVD Seizure Sets Record: The 5,000 Fakes Nabbed in Raids on Two Vancouver Stores Are Worth as Much as $125,000," *The Vancouver Sun*, February 2, 2002.

Criminal Intelligence Service Canada. *Annual Report on Organized Crime Canada.* Ottawa: 1999, 2000, 2001, 2002. <http://www.cics.gc.ca>

Culbert, Lori. "Poolhall Operator Linked to Heroin Ring: A Vancouver Man Is Among 32 People Who Have Been Charged in Connection with Two Cases That Span Several Continents," *The Vancouver Sun*, June 24, 1999.

Dawson, Fabian. "Drug Couriers Linked to Vancouver Jail," *The Vancouver Province*, November 10, 2002.

Derschau, Verana Von. "Defendant: Apartment Was for Meetings," *Associated Press*, February 16, 2001.

"Ducks Lay 'Golden Eggs' in Massive Seizure of Heroin," *Canada Newswire* [Ottawa], September 5, 2000. (Lexis Nexis Document)

Duffy, Andrew. "The Case Against Harkat: CSIS Is Sure the Ottawa Man Is an al-Qaeda Sleeper," December 21, 2002, B1. (Lexis Nexis Document)

Duffy, Andrew. "CSIS Spies to Testify at U.S. Trial: In North American First, Agents Will Give Evidence Against Alleged Terrorist," *The Ottawa Citizen*, February 7, 2002, A5.

Edwards, Peter. "Refugee Found Linked to Terrorism," *Toronto Star*, April 11, 2003, A14.

Fong, Petti. "Alleged Smuggler Allowed Home: Lai Changxing and Wife Released Despite Claims About False Passports," *The Vancouver Sun* [Vancouver], June 29, 2002.

Geddes, John. "The Terrorists Next Door," *Maclean's* [Toronto], September 24, 2001.

Godfrey, Tom. "Hookers Pipeline Through Canada to the U.S.," *The Toronto Sun*, February 17, 2001.

"Government Reports on Vietnamese, Chinese Crime Gangs," *Paris AFP (North European Service) in English*, August 20, 1999 (FBIS Document FTS19990820001434).

Gribbin, Austin. "Global Crime Syndicates Target U.S. From Canada," *Insights on the News*, February 19, 2001.

"Guns and Grenades," *Canada and the World Backgrounder* [Canada], December 2002. (Library of Congress InfoTrac OneFile)

Harder, James D. "Canada Targeted By China Agents," *Insight on the News* [Washington], December 18, 2000. (Library of Congress InfoTrac OneFile)

Heinzl, Mark. "Organized Crime Begins Using Canada as a Base for Operations Ranging From Drugs to Car Theft," *Wall Street Journal*, July 6, 1998, A12.

"Heroin Threatens Recent Drug Gains," *The Bangkok Post*, July 16, 2002.

Hill, John. "Triad Societies Seek Increased Opportunities as China Opens Up," *Jane's Intelligence Review*, January 1, 2003. <http://www.janes.com>

Hogben, David. "Warehouse in Richmond Yields 70 Kilos of High-Grade Heroin: Arrest of Five a Major Blow to Organized Crime, Police Say," *The Vancouver Sun*, January 20, 1999, B1.

Humphreys, Adrian. "Criminals May Be Casing Canada's Diamond Trade," *National Post* [Toronto], August 24, 2002, A10.

Ivens, Andy. "14 Years for Trafficker Nabbed in Heroin Bust," *The Vancouver Province*, February 2, 2001. (Lexis Nexis Document)

Kari, Shannon. "Mother, 50, Sentenced to 17 Years for Smuggling Heroin, Amphetamines: Son, 22, Confesses to Lesser Charge," *The Ottawa Citizen*, June 1, 2002. (LexisNexis Document)

Kelly, Jack. "Quick, Easy Crossing a Thing of the Past at Canadian Border," *Pittsburgh Post-Gazette*, October 14, 2001.

Kingstone, Johnathan. "Feds Ignore Spies Police Source Tells Sun Espionage By China Is Looting Canada of Hi-Tech Secrets," *The Toronto Sun*, April 30, 2000. (LexisNexis Document)

Lamberti, Rob. "Accused Linked to Asian Gangster," *The Toronto Sun*, January 1, 2003.

Library of Congress. Congressional Research Service. CRS Report for Congress. *Trafficking in Women and Children: The U.S. and International Response*. March 18, 2002. <http://fpc.state.gov/documents/organization/9107.pdf>

Lindberg, Kirsten. "Emerging Organized Crime in Chicago," *International Review of Law, Computers & Technology*, July 1998.

Lynch, Jim. "A New Bond at Border," *The Oregonian* [Portland], October 28, 2001, A1.

Lynch, Jim. "U.S., Canada Move to Bolster Borders Against Terrorism," *Newhouse News Service* [Washington], October 26, 2001.

Martin, Susan. "Dreams Ending in Nightmares," *Newsday*, March 11, 2001.

McClelland, Susan. "Inside the Sex Trade: Trafficking in Foreign Prostitutes Is One of the Fastest-Growing Illicit Activities in the World. Welcome to a Hidden Canada—and Lives of Quiet Desperation," *Maclean's* [Toronto], December 3, 2001. (Library of Congress InfoTrac OneFile)

McDonald, Lynn. "Migrant Sex Workers From Eastern Europe and the Former Soviet Union: The Canadian Case," *Center for Applied Social Research, University of Toronto*, November 2000. <http://www.swc-cfc.gc.ca/pubs/0662653351/index_e.html>

Mintz, John. "Fake-ID Arrest Led to FBI Hunt," *Washington Post*, January 3, 2003, A2.

Nasir, Sohail Abdul. "Americans Like to Think the War in Afghanistan Is Over, But That Would Be a Serious Mistake," Turkistan Newsletter, March/April 2003.

Nathanson Centre for the Study of Organized Crime and Corruption. *"A Quarterly Summary,"* January to March 2002, July to September 2002. Toronto. Website: <http://www.yorku.ca/nathanson/>

Nickerson, Colin. "Canada Gets Reputation as a Haven for Fugitives," *Boston Globe*, December 21, 2000, A1.

Nickerson, Colin. "Terror Ties To Canada Highlight a US Concern," *Boston Globe*, June 13, 2002, A1.

Nuttal-Smith, Chris. "B.C. Singled Out by CIA Report on Prostitution: Law Enforcement Officials Worry That Established Sex Trade Gangs Are Making New Links to Organized Crime," *The Vancouver Sun*, April 14, 2000.

Organized Crime Agency of British Columbia. *Annual Report, 2001.* <http://www.ocabc.org/>

Passas, Nikos. *Transnational Crime*. Brookfield: Ashgate, 1999.

Passchier, Lorraine. "Canada Shifts into Overdrive," *CTVNEWS* [Canada], October 15, 2002.

"PNP Hit for Slow Probe of Ho," *Manila Standard*, March 22, 2000. (Lexis Nexis document)

"Police Say Calgary Headquarters of Counterfeit Credit Card Operation, *Canadian Press Newswire*, January 31, 2002. (LexisNexis Document)

Pomfret, John. "Made Man in China Has Gangland Ties, Party Pals," *Seattle Times*, January 21, 2001, A16.

Priest, Dana. "Canadians Hunt al-Qaeda Loyalists," *Milwaukee Journal Sentinel*, December 26, 2002.

Priest, Dana. "Canadian 'Sleepers' in Contact With U.S. Cells," *Toronto Star*, December 26, 2002.

Richard, Amy O'Neill. *International Trafficking in Women to the United States: A Contemporary Manifestation of Slavery and Organized Crime*. Center for the Study of Intelligence, November 1999.

Robinson, Jeffrey. *The Merger: How Organized Crime Is Taking Over Canada and the World*. Toronto: McClelland & Stewart, 1999.

Robinson, Sean. "Northern Border Exposure; Increased Presence of Terrorists in Canada, Staffing Shortage at U.S. Border Patrol a Bad Combination," *The News Tribune* [Tacoma], September 29, 2002.

Royal Canadian Mounted Police, Criminal Intelligence Program. "Drug Situation in Canada – 1999, 2001." Ottawa 2000. <http://www.rcmp-grc.gc.ca>

Runciman, Bob. "Suspected Terrorist Cell Flees Ontario," *Buffalo News*, May 26, 2002, A9.

Schiller, Bill. "Egypt to Toronto: Al Jihad Casts Wide Net," *Toronto Star*, October 21, 2001, A1.

Smith, Paul J. "The Terrorists and Crime Bosses Behind the Fake Passport Trade," *Jane's Intelligence Review*, July 1, 2001.

Statement of James W. Ziglar Before the Senate Appropriations Committee on Treasury and General Government, October 3, 2001.
http://www.immigration.gov/graphics/aboutus/congress/testimonies/2001/10_03_01.pdf

Stinson, Scott. "FBI Hunting for Five From Canada: Agency Believes Men Crossed Border From North, Have Information on Terrorist Threat," *National Post* [Toronto], December 30, 2002, A1.

Sullivan, John P. "Gangs, Hooligans and Anarchists—The Vanguard of Netwar in the Streets." Washington: RAND, 2000. <http://www.rand.org/publications/MR/MR1382/MR1382.ch4.pdf>

"The Mounties Get Cracking," *Maclean's* [Toronto], September 18, 2000. (Library of Congress InfoTrac OneFile)

The Protection Project. *A Human Rights Report on Trafficking of Persons, Especially Women and Children.* Washington: 2002. < http://www.protectionproject.org/>

Thompson, Allan. "Canadian Senate Report Says Ports 'Fertile Ground' for Terrorists, Notes Workers' Criminal Records," *The Toronto Star*, March 2, 2002 (FBIS Document EUP20020304000245).

Timmerman, Kenneth R. "Canadian Border Open to Terrorists," *Insight on the News* [Washington], December 17, 2001. (Library of Congress InfoTrac OneFile).

"Triad Link Alleged in Transfer of Millions to Accused Smuggler Lai," *Beijing China Daily* [Beijing], December 4, 2000 (FBIS Document CPP20001204000045).

"Turks Nab 3 Suspected of Plotting Attack in Israel," *The Vancouver Sun*, February 20, 2002. A12.

"Twelve People Charged in Major Fake Credit Card, Drug Smuggling Ring," *Canadian Press Newswire*, July 3, 2002. (LexisNexis Document)

United States. Department of State. *Country Reports on Human Rights Practices, 2001.* Washington. <http://www.state.gov>

United States. Department of State. *Patterns of Global Terrorism, 2002.* Washington: 2003. <http://www.state.gov>

"Wa Link to Triad Confirmed," *The Bangkok Post*, December 22, 2000.

Wallace, Bill. "Chinese Crime Ring Muscles In," *San Francisco Chronicle*, December 1, 1997.

Walters, Joan. "Criminals Support Terrorists; Organized Crime Provides Forged ID," *Hamilton Spectator* [Ontario], November 2, 2001.

Weisman, Jonathan. "Cigarette Black Market Feared; Canadian Tax Increase Led to Smuggling and Organized Crime Rivalry; Industry Complicity Alleged," *The Sun* [Baltimore], May 10, 1998.

Woo, Lora Jo. "Asian American Women: Issues, Concerns, and Responsive Human and Civil Rights Advocacy." New York: Ford Foundation, 2002.

Yang, Hsiao. "China Steps Up Its Crackdown on the Mob and Severely Punishes Mob Leaders," *Hong Kong Kuang Chiao Ching*, February 16, 2001 (FBIS Document CPP20010216000052).